PETS MAZES

Becky Radtke

DOVER PUBLICATIONS, INC.
Mineola, New York

Bibliographical Note

Pets Mazes is a new work, first published by
Dover Publications, Inc., in 2004.

International Standard Book Number
ISBN-13: 978-0-486-43524-4
ISBN-10: 0-486-43524-5

Manufactured in the United States by Courier Corporation
43524508
www.doverpublications.com

Note

Each pet in this little book is on its way somewhere, and you will help it get there! Just draw a line from the beginning arrow to the finish arrow in each maze. You will find the way for a Persian cat to get to her toy mouse, lead three parakeets to their exercise ladder, guide an iguana to its heat lamp, and much more!

Try to complete all of the 48 mazes before checking the Solutions, which begin on page 52. For even more fun, color in the finished mazes with crayons or colored pencils. Now it's time to meet the pets!

Peter Pooch needs to get back to the farm. Help him find a path through the cornfields.

4

This Persian cat, Penelope, wants to play with her toy mouse. Help her find the way.

5

Help Paula Poodle find the way to her grooming brush.
Pick up three hair bows along the way.

Lucy got an award in the Lop rabbit contest. Help her find the right path to her award.

Help Snowy, a Siamese cat, find the path to the big ball of yarn. He's in the mood to play!

8

Pat, a praying mantis, drinks water from a spoon. Please
show her the path to reach it.

Bobby Basset Hound has a brand new collar! Find the
path for him to follow to reach it.

10

Please help Mindy, a tailless Manx cat, get to her kittens. The letters tell what they are saying.

Help this pet snake get to his tank. Along the way you will find letters to spell his name.

12

Barney Bulldog is on his way home. Help him get there, and pick up three toys along the way.

Oliver, an Oriental Shorthair cat, wants to stretch out on the rug. Find the path to get there.

Gwen the guinea pig is thirsty. Please show her the way to get to her water bottle.

15

Boots, a Snowshoe cat, is ready for some tuna! Help him find the way there.

16

Larry and Lois, a pair of lovebirds, want to meet. Help Lois get to Larry.

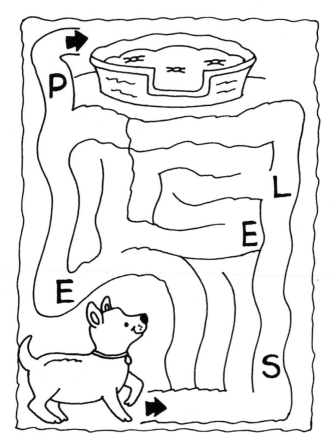

Help Carly Chihuahua get to her bed. The letters spell what she will do when she gets there.

18

Hubert saw some nice fish in the pet store. Help him find the way there.

Harold Hamster has lots of energy. Find the path for him to get to his exercise wheel.

These three parakeets love to climb! Find the way for them to get to the ladder.

King, an American Eskimo dog, wants his dinner! Find the way for him to get to his food bowl.

Sue, a spotted salamander, can smell those delicious leaves!
Show her the way to get to them.

Min loves it when her Yorkshire Terrier, Prudence, sits in her lap. Help Prudence get to Min.

24

Pixie the pony is prancing off to her stable. Help Pixie by showing her the right path.

Paul, a potbellied pig, sleeps on the floor in Jane's room. Find the way for him to get there.

26

Ben has something for Hal the hermit crab. Show Ben the way and find out what he has.

When you find the path from Polly Parrot to Mickey, you will spell out what Polly says.

Tina Tarantula loves to hide in the broken flowerpot. Find the path that she takes to get to it.

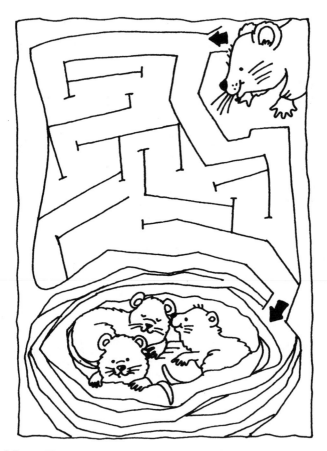

Mama Rat wants to check on her babies. Show her the right path to get to them.

Gary the Gecko wants to reach the waiting hands of his owner, Hannah. Help Gary get there.

Clancy Cockatiel would love to swing on his perch. Help him find the right path.

32

Don, a bearded dragon, is on his way to the warm water in the sink. Show him the right path.

Joe the jumping spider has escaped! Please help him find the way back to his jar.

34

Take Tammy Tree Frog along the right path to this nice branch. It's one of her favorite places.

Help Fran and Fred Ferret find the way to the ball so that they can play.

Clyde Caterpillar is ready to change himself. Find the right path to see what he becomes.

Cathy Chameleon wants to get to the drinking water sprayed in her cage. Help her reach it.

38

Let's see how much Stanley, a Saint Bernard, weighs. Find the right path to the scale.

Help Carlos Canary follow the musical notes from his singing to the box of birdseed.

These zebra fish see their food floating on top of the water.
Help them find the way there.

Ted Turtle wants to play in the grass. Find the right path for him to take.

Show Brenda Bunny the path to get to Patty. Brenda can nibble the carrots on the way.

These tropical fish love to hide inside the castle! Show them the way.

44

Please help Ginny Gerbil find the right way to her mirror.
Follow the hearts along the path.

Isaac the Iguana likes to sit near the heat lamp. Show him the right path to get there.

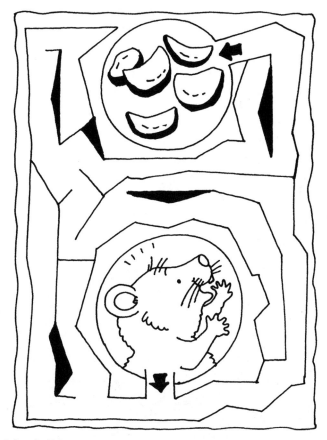

Morris Mouse smells apples, one of his favorite treats.
Help Morris find the way to the apple bits.

Alice Ant wants to join her friends in the ant farm. Would you show her the way?

48

Chinchillas take "dust baths," and Chuck is ready for his. Please take him to the bowl.

Sammy Schnauzer is headed home. Can you show him the path?

50

Amy would like to take a closer look at Walt Walkingstick.
Won't you show her the way?

51

Solutions

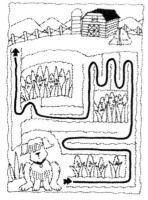

Page 4

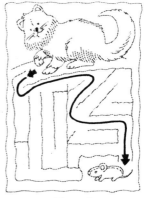

Page 5

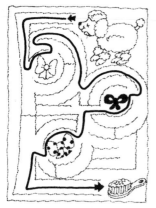

Page 6

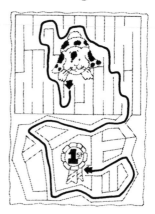

Page 7

Page 8

Page 9

Page 10

Page 11

53

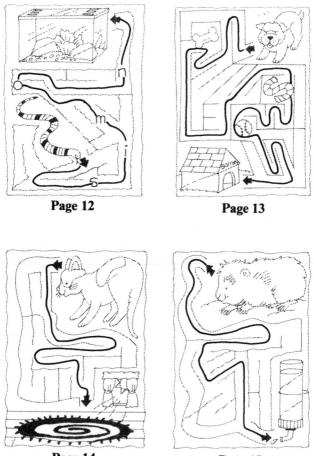

Page 12

Page 13

Page 14

Page 15

54

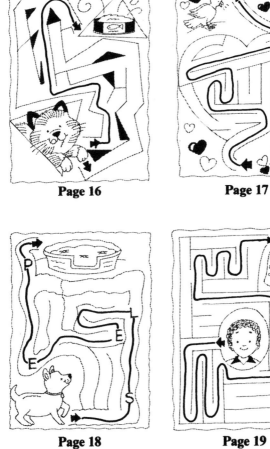

Page 16

Page 17

Page 18

Page 19

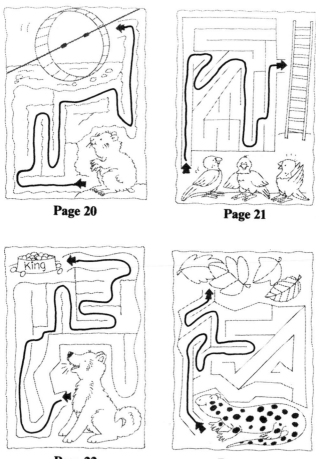

Page 20

Page 21

Page 22

Page 23

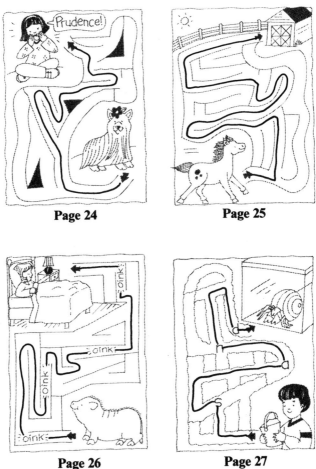

Page 24

Page 25

Page 26

Page 27

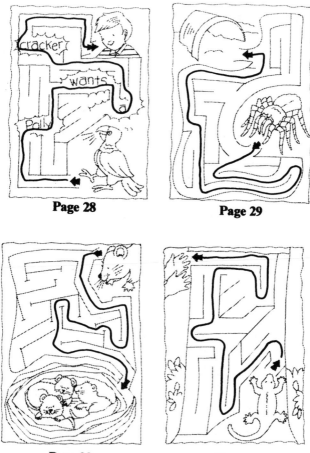

Page 28

Page 29

Page 30

Page 31

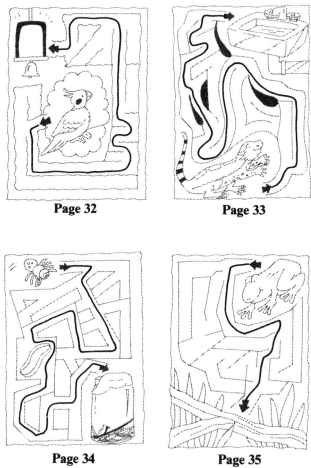

Page 32

Page 33

Page 34

Page 35

Page 36

Page 37

Page 38

Page 39

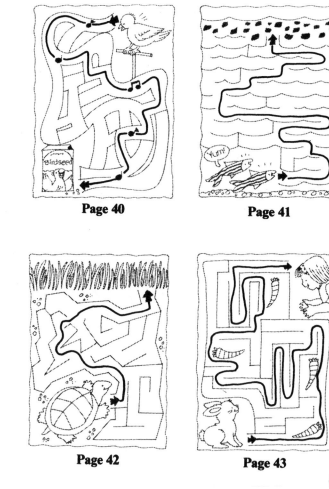

Page 40

Page 41

Page 42

Page 43

Page 44

Page 45

Page 46

Page 47

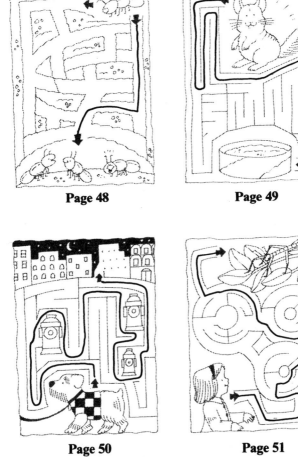

Page 48

Page 49

Page 50

Page 51